THE LITTLE BOOK OF
CONFIDENCE

SUSAN JEFFERS

RIDER

LONDON · SYDNEY · AUCKLAND · JOHANNESBURG

21 23 25 27 29 30 28 26 24 22

Copyright © Susan Jeffers 1999

All rights reserved. No part of this publication may be
reproduced, stored in a retrieval system, or transmitted
in any form or by any means, electronic, mechanical,
photocopying, recording or otherwise, without the
prior permission of the copyright owner.

First published in 1999 by Rider, an imprint of
Ebury Publishing,

Random House, 20 Vauxhall Bridge Road,
London SW1V 2SA

www.randomhouse.co.uk

The Random House Group Limited supports
The Forest Stewardship Council (FSC), the leading internationa
forest certification organisation. All our titles that are printed o
Greenpeace approved FSC certified paper carry the FSC logo.
Our paper procurement policy can be found
at www.rbooks.co.uk/environment

The Random House Group Limited Reg. No. 954009

Papers used by Rider are natural, recyclable products
made from wood grown in sustainable forests.

Printed and bound by Leo Paper Products Ltd.

A CIP catalogue record for this book is available from
the British Library
ISBN 9780712608268

INTRODUCTION

Confidence...where does it come
from? It comes from the knowledge
that within you lies an immense
amount of power and love to create
all that you will ever need in life.
That's confidence! The problem is
we too often seem to forget! This
little book of confidence is meant to
be a constant reminder and,
thankfully, it can be carried with you
wherever you go.

Inside, you will recognize in capsule
form the life-changing tools
embodied in *Feel the Fear and Do It*

Anyway and *Feel the Fear...and Beyond.*
And as you go through this little
book over and over again, you will
imprint upon your mind the
empowering thoughts that allow your
confidence to grow and grow and
grow. So read it often, especially
when you are facing new situations
in your life.

Inspiration will be at your fingertips
as you learn how to embrace life
fully with a feeling of courage, trust,
fulfilment and joy. Enjoy!
From my heart to yours,

Susan Jeffers

TAKE THE

HIGH ROAD

THE HIGHER SELF

Inside you is a place filled
with joy, creativity, intuition,
peace, power, love and all
good things. I call it the
Higher Self. Whenever in this
place, your confidence soars
and all seems right with
the world.

THE LOWER SELF

Inside you is also a place filled with self-doubt, fear, anger, helplessness, scarcity and all negative things. This is the Lower Self. Whenever in this place, your confidence disappears and all seems wrong with the world.

LOWER-SELF THINKING IS A HABIT

Yes, Lower-Self thinking is only a habit. The good news is that habits can be broken. By practising a Higher-Self way of thinking, your fear diminishes and your confidence rises.

BECOME A HIGHER-SELF THINKER

Your task is set before you...
it is to take the steps necessary
to become a Higher-Self
thinker. Many of these steps
are embodied in this little
book of confidence.

HOW DO I KNOW IF I AM THINKING 'HIGH'?

When you are thinking thoughts of joy, creativity, intuition, peace, power, love and all good things, you are in the world of the Higher Self.

HOW DO I KNOW IF I AM THINKING 'LOW'?

When you are thinking thoughts of self-doubt, fear, anger, helplessness, scarcity and all negative things, you can be sure you are in the world of the Lower Self. And it's time to find the High road.

AWARENESS
IS A GOOD
START

MEET THE CHATTERBOX!

I call the voice of the Lower Self, the *Chatterbox*. It sounds like this: 'I'm not good enough.' 'I'll never get ahead.' 'Everyone else does it better than me.' Or any other thought that takes away your confidence.

HELP! I CAN'T SHUT IT UP!

Once you are aware of the Chatterbox, you can't seem to shut it up. When you are lying in bed, showering, driving, eating or whatever, the Chatterbox tries to drive you crazy with fearful thoughts.

AWARENESS LETS YOU KNOW IT'S TIME FOR ACTION

Once you are aware of the Chatterbox, at last you can do something about it (even if it is driving you crazy!). When you are unaware of this mischievous little voice, you are at its mercy.

DROWN OUT THE CHATTERBOX

It's so simple. To quiet the Chatterbox, commit to replacing it with the voice of the Higher Self which always tells you that you are good enough and pulls you up into the best of who you are.

AFFIRM

THE BEST

POSITIVE AFFIRMATIONS: A WONDERFUL TOOL

An affirmation is a strong, positive statement telling you that 'all is well'. With constant repetition, affirmations help you drown out the negative messages of the Chatterbox. Confidence restored!

AFFIRMATIONS WORK

Just saying, thinking or writing positive thoughts make us stronger in every way...body, mind and spirit...whether we believe the words or not. They calm and heal the scared child within. MAGIC!

'IT'S ALL HAPPENING PERFECTLY'

Repeat this affirmation over and over again. It is a shortened version of: 'Even if things are not going the way I want them to go, I will simply trust that all things happen for a reason and I will learn and grow from it all.

'I'LL HANDLE IT'

Repeating this affirmation can give you an enormous sense of peace when the frightening 'What Ifs' come up in your life. 'What if I lose my money? I'll handle it.' 'What if I get sick? I'll handle it.' You really can handle *whatever* life brings you.

ACTING-AS-IF

Affirmations are a form of 'acting-as-if'. If you act-as-if long enough, your mind lets in the *possibility* that it is so. And ultimately, it *is* so. Constantly tell yourself: 'I am powerful and loving and I have nothing to fear.' Then watch your confidence grow.

REPETITION
IS THE KEY

As you use your affirmations over and over again, you will notice that little-by-little the voice of the Higher Self will get louder and louder while the voice of the Lower Self gets softer and softer.

What a relief!

NOTICE THE CHANGES

When you repeat affirmations over and over again, not only do subtle changes occur within you, altering for the better the way you act and feel, but the world reacts to you in a more positive way.

IN COMES THE GOOD

As you become more powerful and loving, you draw healthier people into your life. Like attracts like. The more positive you are, the greater the positive energy you draw into your life.

MAKE AFFIRMATIONS A PART OF YOUR LIFE

Experiment until you find affirmations that feel right to you at any given time. Then surround yourself with these positive thoughts...on your desk, your mirror...or wherever you will be reminded about how powerful and loving you truly are.

TRUST YOUR HIGHER SELF

Your Higher Self always tells you the truth: 'You have nothing to fear.' Your Lower Self always tells you the big lie: 'You have everything to fear.' Which voice would you rather listen to?

'WHAT WOULD MY HIGHER SELF SAY?'

Whenever you feel worried
about something in life,
'role-play' what your Higher
Self would say about the
situation. Then write down the
answer. You will know if it is
the voice of the Higher Self if
it reminds you in some form
or another, 'Not to worry.
All is well.'

'I LET GO...
AND I TRUST'

Letting go and trusting in the Grand Design and your Higher Self brings a sense of relief. Repeating the affirmation 'I let go...and I trust' over and over again will remind you to look for the blessings in all life experiences.

KEEP PRACTISING!

New challenges confront us every day of our lives. It serves us well to practise our favourite affirmations daily to keep us in the realm of the Higher Self. What a wonderful place to spend the rest of our lives!

LET GO OF

OUTCOMES

IT MAY HAPPEN...OR IT MAY NOT

There is nothing wrong with creating clear, detailed pictures of how you want your life to be, but it is essential to add one vital Higher Self element to your visualization, and that is... *let go of the outcome!*

LETTING GO
SETS YOU FREE

If whatever you visualize
happens, so be it. If it doesn't
happen, so be it. You will
handle it all in a powerful and
loving way. When you are able
to think in this Higher-Self
way, you have discovered the
meaning of freedom in the
highest sense.

THE HIGHER-SELF 'QUALIFIER'

As you set any of your future goals, end with the Higher-Self 'qualifier' as in the following example:
'By this time next year, I will be married... *or whatever else the Grand Design has in store for me. It's all happening perfectly for my Highest good.*'

SAY 'YES'

TO LIFE

CHOOSE YOUR REACTIONS TO IT ALL

Whatever cards life may deal you, however bad things may seem, you can choose how you react. No one can ever take away your *reaction* to your experiences in life.

'YES' IS THE MAGIC WORD

Right now, nod your head up and down and softly say YES. YES is more than a word, it is the essence of Higher-Self thinking. It says, 'No matter what happens in my life, I'll make something wonderful out of it.'

YOU CAN SAY 'YES' TO ANYTHING

Although they may not be immediately obvious, blessings can always be found in even the worst and most frightening of situations, *if you look for them.* I said 'YES' to breast cancer and it made all the difference in the world.

SAYING 'YES' MEANS FOCUSING ON THE POSITIVE

There is enormous power in looking for the good in any situation in which you may find yourself. It certainly beats looking for the bad!

POSITIVE THINKING WORKS!

Some people make fun of positive thinking. Why would they prefer to look at the gloom instead of the light? Thinking positively transforms your experience of life...for the better. It makes sense, doesn't it?

SAYING 'YES' IS NOT ABOUT DENIAL

Seeing life in a positive, life-affirming way is not to deny negative feelings such as fear and pain. Bad times are an unavoidable part of life. To acknowledge our pain is very important to a healthy life.

SAY 'YES' TO
IT ALL

Real positive thinking is saying
YES even to the fear and pain
– realizing you will always get
to the other side. And when
you reach the other side, you
notice your confidence has
grown enormously.

SAYING 'YES' GIVES MEANING TO LIFE

Saying YES to life's challenges creates a deeper meaning and purpose in your life. It allows you to understand the pain and fear that others feel and creates a connection to everyone around you. Your compassion grows.

MAKE

NO-LOSE

DECISIONS

THE NO-LOSE PHILOSOPHY

'I can't lose — regardless of the outcome of the decision I make. I look forward to the opportunities for learning and growing that either choice gives me. Any road I take is strewn with riches for my Highest good.'

THERE ARE NO MISTAKES

Don't worry that the 'wrong' decision will deprive you of something – money, friends, status, lovers or whatever the 'right' decision is supposed to bring you. Remember, if you learn through your 'mistakes', there are no mistakes!

DO YOUR HOMEWORK

Before a decision is made,
there is homework to do.
Establish your priorities, find
out all you can about various
alternatives, talk to others,
learn as much
as you can.

TRUST YOUR INSTINCTS

When all the homework is done, pay attention to your intuition...your gut feeling. You will be surprised at the good advice your subconscious can give...when you listen.

MAKE ALL DECISIONS 'RIGHT' DECISIONS

Remember, as long as you learn and grow, you can't lose. The No-Lose approach to decision-making guarantees that all your decisions will be the *right* decisions.

ACCEPT RESPONSIBILITY FOR YOUR DECISIONS

Do not blame others if things do not work out to your liking. Blame is a powerless act. If you see all your decisions as right decisions, it will be much easier to take responsibility for them!

KNOW WHEN TO CHANGE COURSE

Commit yourself to any decision you make, but if you see it isn't right for you, then change course. The trick in life is not to worry about making a wrong decision, it's knowing when to correct.

WHEN IS IT TIME TO CORRECT?

Confusion and dissatisfaction are clues that you are off course in some way and need to change direction. Did you ever think that confusion and dissatisfaction could be positive feelings? Now you know they can be.

LIGHTEN UP

When we realize that all that happens is for our Highest good, we understand the wonderful saying...'Don't sweat the small stuff...and it's all small stuff.'

THE ULTIMATE CONFIDENCE

Remember to say to yourself
with great frequency:
'Whatever happens as a result
of my decisions...I'LL
HANDLE IT! And you
definitely will!

RECLAIM

YOUR POWER

LET GO OF THE VICTIM MENTALITY

The victim mentality is a product of our Lower Self. When you play the role of victim, you give away your power. When you take responsibility for your life, your power is restored.

YOU ARE IN CONTROL

Because you can learn to control your *reactions* to whatever life gives you, you have the upper hand. You can create your own misery...or you can create your own joy. That's power!

HOW TO TAKE RESPONSIBILITY

Taking responsibility for your own experience of life means never blaming anyone else for anything you are doing, being, having or feeling.

DON'T BLAME YOURSELF

The path to greater confidence and self-fulfilment is a lengthy process of trial and error. There is no need to blame yourself for your past, present or future behaviour. It is all part of the learning process.

UNCOVER THE PAYOFFS

Once you can discover the underlying payoffs – the reasons why you remain 'stuck' in certain negative situations – it's much easier to move on. *Awareness helps us to take action.*

ARE YOU A COMPLAINER?

Complaining is a very common activity of everyone's Lower Self. Complaining is also a big clue that you are not taking responsibility for your experience of life.

HOW TO STOP COMPLAINING

Complaining for many is such an embedded habit that we don't even notice we are doing it! Enlist the help of a close friend and agree that for one entire week there will be no complaints. You may have very silent conversations!

SO WHAT DO
WE TALK ABOUT?

Talk about all the great things
happening in your life... all the
blessings that surround you.
Keep your conversations
upbeat and filled with
appreciation.

YOU HAVE THE CHOICE

Every waking moment you are choosing how you feel. Are you going to see lack or abundance in your life? Are you going to make yourself miserable or appreciative? It's up to you.

TAKE ACTION

Complaining will not change things in your life; only action will. Make a list of all you need to do to change what doesn't work in your life and, little-by-little, begin making those changes.

'SCULPT' YOUR LIFE

Few sculpt their lives. Most accept what comes their way and then gripe about it. You have the power to create what you need. Commitment, action and positive thoughts will take you a long way.

SPEAK

CONFIDENTLY

WATCH YOUR WORDS

The words you use impact on how you feel about yourself. Certain words are destructive; other are empowering.

CHOOSING IS POWERFUL

The words 'I can't' imply that you are helpless, whereas 'I choose not to' implies confidence and strength.

YOUR SUBCONSCIOUS MIND HEARS

When your subconscious hears messages like 'I can't', it registers 'He's/She's weak.' Replace such weak words with strong words that tell your subconscious mind that you really are in control.

THE VOCABULARY OF POWER

Eliminate negative words from your vocabulary. Replace 'It's terrible' with 'It's a great learning experience', 'It's not my fault' with 'I'm totally responsible', and so on. Not only will your self-esteem improve, so will the way others treat you.

SEE THE GIFTS

Instead of seeing life's obstacles as problems, see them as opportunities, opening the door to growth. Each time you have the opportunity to stretch your capacity to handle the world around you, the more powerful and confident you will feel.

THE KEY
TO SECURITY

People who have been forced
to face their worst fears – and
more – re-emerge much
stronger. Remember, *security
lies not in having things, but
handling things.*

EXPAND

YOUR LIMITS

THE
COMFORT ZONE

Most of us operate within a zone that is comfortable, outside of which we are uncomfortable. For example, you may happily initiate friendships with colleagues, but won't approach the 'higher ups'. Notice what situations in life make you uncomfortable.

START TAKING LITTLE RISKS

Each day take a little risk to expand your comfort zone. Phone someone you feel intimidated about calling. Walk proudly into a restaurant where you are uncomfortable dining alone. Not to worry... you'll handle whatever happens.

WATCH YOUR CONFIDENCE GROW

Each time you move out of your comfort zone, your confidence builds. Your world becomes larger and larger. Expanding your comfort zone becomes easier and easier with each risk, despite any fear you may be experiencing.

YOU ARE

NOT ALONE

EVERYONE
FEELS FEAR

Not only do you experience
fear whenever you are on
unfamiliar territory, so does
everyone else. By virtue of the
fact we are all human beings,
we share similar feelings. Fear
is no exception.

IT ONLY LOOKS LIKE OTHERS HAVE NO FEAR

You may think others – such as celebrities – are lucky because they are not afraid to put themselves out there. *Not so!* They had to push through a tremendous amount of fear to get where they are today...and they are still pushing.

THE FEAR
NEVER GOES AWAY

As long as you keep stretching
your capabilities and
expanding your horizons, you
are going to experience fear.
It's the human condition. But
as your confidence builds, it
will become easier and easier
to 'feel the fear and do it
anyway!'

HANDLING

FEAR

YOUR SECRET FEAR

At the bottom of every one of your fears is simply the fear that you can't handle whatever life may bring you.

TRUST IN YOURSELF

All you have to do to diminish – and alter your relationship with – fear is to develop more trust in your ability to handle what comes your way. You develop trust by taking action.

FEEL THE FEAR...AND DO IT ANYWAY

Often we think, 'I'll do it when I am not so afraid.' But in reality, it works the other way round. The 'doing it' comes *before* the fear goes away. The only way to get rid of the fear of doing something is to go out and do it.

ACTION MAKES THE FEAR GO AWAY

Once you have done something you have feared a number of times, the fear of that particular situation goes away. And it's then time to further expand the comfort zone and move on to the next situation you fear.

EACH STEP TAKES YOU FORWARD

When you fear doing something, and do it anyway, you not only eliminate that particular fear, you get a big bonus – you do a lot towards building your self-confidence.

PAT YOURSELF ON THE BACK

Notice and enjoy the sense of accomplishment you feel with each and every fear you overcome. Giving yourself a pat on the back helps to raise your confidence.

EACH STEP PREPARES YOU FOR THE NEXT

You feel so good once you have felt the fear and done it anyway that before long you will discover something else you want to accomplish. And guess what! The fear begins again. A good sign!

YOU CAN HANDLE IT ALL

As you continue pushing through fear and doing it anyway, you learn to trust your ability to handle whatever life may hand you.
Trust me on this one!

A HIDDEN BENEFIT OF TAKING RISKS

People who refuse to take risks live with a feeling of helplessness which is far more frightening than the fear associated with actually taking a risk. Fear permeates their lives.

NOTE: DON'T TAKE FOOLISH RISKS!!!

Please note that the risks I am talking about do not include physically dangerous acts, or those that infringe on the rights of other people.

THE GREEN LIGHT OF FEAR

Retrain your thinking so you interpret your inappropriate fears as a green light to move ahead – an opportunity to grow and live life more fully – instead of as a signal to retreat.

KEEP REPEATING 'I'LL HANDLE IT'

'Whatever happens to me, given any situation, I'll handle it!' Repeat this to yourself over and over again until you realize that you truly can handle *anything* that comes your way.

WHEN 'THEY' DON'T WANT YOU TO GROW

DON'T BE SURPRISED!

Know that in all likelihood, as you become more confident and start to expand your horizons, you are going to get resistance from people in your life. They feel threatened that you will leave them behind.

MAKE OTHERS
FEEL LOVED

Find win-win ways of handling
negative feedback from others.
Show them that you care. Send
them loving notes, flowers, or
whatever you feel will express
your appreciation that they are
in your life.

REASSURE
YOUR PARTNER

Often is it is your partner
who resists your growth most
of all, threatened by your new-
found confidence and power.
Reassure your mate and give
him or her your support,
but be clear that you are
committed to your
continuing growth.

RISK ROCKING
THE BOAT

When you choose to remain
'stuck' because you do not
want to upset your partner,
you become resentful.
Ultimately the relationship
suffers and the boat rocks
anyway!

BELIEVE YOUR PARTNER WANTS THE BEST FOR YOU

Believe that your partner wants what is best for you and that he or she will ultimately love the positive changes in you. If not, is it a relationship you truly want?

CONFIDENCE AND LOVE GO TOGETHER

As you grow in confidence, so does your capacity for love. Greater confidence diminishes your need for approval. Paradoxically, the less you need someone's approval, the more you are able to love them.

POWER AND LOVE ALSO GO TOGETHER

With a sense of power, love is able to flow. Your heart opens and you can be authentically loving to those around you. Without a sense of power, neediness is created and love is destroyed.

CONFIDENT PEOPLE ARE MAGNETS

As your confidence grows,
you draw beautiful people into
your life. You learn you need
never feel alone.

CREATE A CIRCLE OF FEAR-LESS FRIENDS

A STRONG SUPPORT SYSTEM REALLY HELPS

Cultivate the sort of friends who make you feel good about yourself and who encourage you to 'Go for it!' It is amazingly empowering to have a circle of supportive and loving friends.

WHAT KIND OF FRIENDS DO YOU HAVE?

Think of six friends you have and ask yourself if they are 'Be careful' (Lower Self) friends or 'Go-for-it' (Higher Self) friends. Now you know who to talk to when you want to move forward in your life!

WHAT KIND OF
FRIEND ARE YOU?

Are you a 'Go-for-it' friend
who encourages others to
move forward with their lives
or a 'Be careful' friend,
constantly warning of the
possibility of failure.

BECOME A HIGHER -SELF FRIEND

Friends are a mirror of our own behaviour. Think of a dozen Higher-Self qualities you would like in your friends. Then pick up the mirror and *begin developing these qualities in yourself.*

YES, LIKE ATTRACTS LIKE

As you adopt a more positive approach to life and as your confidence grows, you are automatically drawn to and attract a different kind of person...the Higher-Self kind.

INITIATE
HIGHER-SELF
FRIENDSHIPS

Think of six people you
admire as acquaintances and
would like to get to know as
friends. Then invite them for
lunch or dinner. If someone
says 'no', remember you can
handle it. Then simply go on
to the next one.

MEET NEW HIGHER-SELF FRIENDS

Think of some of the things you would love to try — riding, travelling, politics, photography, personal growth workshops or whatever. Then search for local activities revolving around those interests and sign up. You will meet like-minded souls.

BE YOUR OWN
BEST FRIEND

Break the habit of putting
yourself down. Quiet your
Chatterbox with reassuring
messages of power and love.
Follow the path with the heart
and watch yourself grow into a
confident human being.

GET SOME
BALANCE IN
YOUR LIFE

DON'T SET YOURSELF UP FOR PAIN

If you invest all your emotions in only one aspect of your life, such as relationship, work or children, how do you feel if you experience a loss in that area? *Empty! Lonely! Depressed!*

DEPENDENCY IS UNHEALTHY

When you make anything or anybody the focus of your whole life, you create a deep-seated fear of losing it. Ironically, your neediness often makes you lose what you most want to hold on to.

SPREAD IT AROUND

When you spread your emotional investment, you enrich your whole experience of life and your confidence grows. You also protect yourself against the pain of loss. The result? Your fears are greatly diminished.

YOUR
SAFETY NET

CREATE A FEAR-LESS GRID OF YOUR LIFE

Draw a square which represents your whole life. Then divide it into nine boxes, each representing a different area of your life such as personal growth, relationship, career, family, spiritual growth, friends, contribution to the community, alone time and play time.

'CONTRIBUTION' IS IMPORTANT

We all have a deep desire to spread our love into this world. When we contribute to the well-being of the world around us, we become stronger. We become the giver, instead of the taker, and our confidence not only grows, it soars!

'SPIRITUALITY' IS ALSO IMPORTANT

Make the Higher-Self tools you are now learning an integral part of your everyday life. These tools will keep you centred and move you from a place of fear to a place of love, power and trust in the world. Put 'spirituality' in the centre of your Grid of Life. It then radiates to every area of your life.

THE LOOK OF YOUR LIFE

After you have filled in the nine boxes of your Grid of Life, ask yourself how you want each of these areas to look. Take time to think about it. Then make a list and – step-by-step – take appropriate action!

NOW YOU ARE SAFE

When your grid of life is full
and balanced, a loss in any one
area doesn't wipe you out. Yes,
there's a little hole in your
heart and that hurts. But the
loss doesn't wipe you out.
There is so much richness in
the rest of your life.

YOU ARE TRULY IMPORTANT

If you have many things in your life, but one area — such as your relationship, work or child — is of all-consuming importance, enhance your commitment to *all* the other areas of your life. You are important to this world and you deserve a rich life.

THE
ESSENTIAL
EXTRAS

COMMIT 100% TO ALL AREAS OF YOUR LIFE

When you are with your family, be *with* them 100% – not reviewing work, not reading the papers, or wishing you were somewhere else. When you are at work, give it all you've got, holding nothing back. Give 100% as you participate in all areas of your life.

WHAT HAPPENS WHEN YOU GIVE 100%?

When you commit to giving 100% to all areas of your life, your sense of focus, excitement, participation, enjoyment, fulfilment and happiness come alive, perhaps for the first time. What a glorious feeling that is!

GIVING 100% DOES NOT MEAN FOREVER

Life is always bringing us new adventures. New challenges arise involving career moves; relationships may end, and so on. But if you have given 100%, when the time comes to move on, there is nothing to regret.

KNOW THAT YOU COUNT

Know your presence makes a difference in all areas of your life. If you don't understand that your life really does make a difference, *act-as-if you do make a difference!*

THE ACT–AS–IF QUESTION

The act–as–if question is 'What would I be doing if I were really important in all areas of my life?' When you ask yourself this powerful question, you will come up with some pretty powerful and exciting answers.

LIVE THE ACT-AS-IF WAY

As you answer the act-as-if question, begin acting on the answers you get. As you do what you would do if you were really important, you eventually 'live into' the realization that *you really are important in this very needy world.*
(Read this again!)

THE MAGIC DUO

Knowing that you count and *100% commitment* are the 'Magic duo'. They are the extra ingredients you need to make the Grid of Life fill you up on a deep emotional level. Together they create magical results.

USING THE
GRID OF LIFE

MAKE A PLAN OF ACTION

For each area of your life space, ask yourself 'What would I be doing if I really counted?' Make a list. And then begin doing what's on your list. Remember: *you are creating your life.*

MAKE IT OFFICIAL!

To make it official, write in
your daily diary one or more
actions you want to take in
each area of your nine-boxed
grid... your life space. You can
see the richness in your life
growing with each action
you take.

BE FLEXIBLE

Don't worry if you don't cover every item every day. If you have a deadline, or if a child is sick, or if you are on holiday, other areas of your life will have to take a back seat for a while. Remember, you are creating an 'attitude' of fullness...not more pressure!

LIFE IS HUGE!

Your Fear-Less Grid of Life embodies an attitude of fullness, confidence and action. When you realize how rich your life truly is, little can take away from your sense of well-being. Always remember, *life is huge!* Enjoy it all!

OPEN YOUR

EYES TO

ABUNDANCE

THE ART OF GRATITUDE

The art of gratitude is being able to make ordinary things in your life extraordinary. Write or think of *fifty* extraordinary ordinary things for which you are truly grateful. And do this every night before you go to sleep. Life is not only huge, it is also rich!

REMEMBER THE BRIGHT SIDE

Train yourself to stop complaining and look for the blessings and beauty that surrounds you every moment of every day, despite what is happening in any particular situation in your life.

AFFIRM THE ABUNDANCE

Whenever you feel scarcity and fear – about money, resources, beauty, love or anything else--repeat this affirmation: *'My life is rich and full. I am focusing on all the beauty within and around me.'*

GIVE IT AWAY!

DO YOU GIVE OR DO YOU SIMPLY EXCHANGE?

Most of us operate on a hidden barter system. Few genuinely ever give away anything without expecting something in return – money, appreciation, love or whatever.

WHEN GIVING IS ABOUT GETTING, FEAR IS CREATED

If getting is your motivation for giving, you worry about not getting anything back. Then you worry about not getting back *enough*. Your fear of being shortchanged or taken advantage of destroys your peace of mind.

GENUINE GIVING

When you give with an open
heart, with nothing expected
in return, peace reigns.
Genuine giving creates joy
within our being. Genuine
giving is a great boost to our
confidence.

BE OTHER-INVOLVED

As we take the attention off the self, we can give from a place of love rather than a place of expectation. This is freedom in the Highest sense.

THE PARADOX OF GENUINE GIVING

When we give genuinely, with thought only for others, we often find that more comes back to us than we could ever have imagined.

GIVING DIMINISHES FEAR

When you focus on giving, you lose your neediness and you feel 'full-filled'. As you give, your sense of power and love gets greater and greater and greater.

SAYING THANK YOU... OFTEN!

Make a list of all the significant people in your life. Then systematically go about thanking them for all they have contributed to your well-being. The words 'Thank you' are two of the most powerful ... and giving words ever spoken.

GIVE OF
YOURSELF

When you help others, you
become powerful. And when
others use what they have
learned from you, your effect
in the world is greatly
magnified.

GIVE AWAY PRAISE

Often the people we find most difficult to praise are those closest to us. Yet praise is a wonderful way of releasing anger and resentment. Praise can take down the barriers to love and connection.

GIVE AWAY MONEY

Money – no matter how
wealthy one may be – is a
huge issue for many people.
Within reason, begin to give
money away to those in need.
Know that you will always
find a way to create whatever
you need.

YOUR HIGHER PURPOSE IS TO BE A GIVER

In whatever you do in life, rise above the petty details and find the many ways to give to the world around you. In so doing, you will receive so much... most of all, the confidence that your life really makes a difference.

ONE STEP

AT A TIME

PRACTICE MAKES PERFECT

Just as you need to exercise your muscles to keep in great physical shape, so you have to exercise the muscles that keep you in your Higher Self. With enough practice, Higher-Self thinking will dominate.

TRUST THAT ALL IS HAPPENING PERFECTLY

Sometimes we don't realize
that change is occurring
within us. Trust that as you use
your Higher-Self tools, you are
becoming a more powerful,
loving and confident human
being. Little by little, glimmers
of confidence will happily
be seen... and embraced.

BE PATIENT!

You are on the right path. Be
patient knowing that as you do
your Higher-Self exercises, a
greater confidence is building
within you. Patience is
knowing growth will
happen...and giving it time to
happen. Notice that a flower
blooms when it's ready to
bloom.

PAT YOURSELF ON THE BACK

The most negative thing you can do is to let your Lower Self berate you for not doing it 'right', or fast enough or whatever! The most positive thing you can do is pat yourself on the back for every little step you take.

COMMIT TO SPIRITUAL GROWTH

The powerful tools in this book – affirmations, saying YES to life, letting go of outcomes, making no-lose decisions and others – open us up to Higher-Self thinking. Think of them as food for the body, mind and soul – and don't forget to eat regularly.

YOU ARE ON THE RIGHT PATH

Listen to the best of who you are...the voice that always reminds you that you are powerful and loving and have nothing to fear. You are a person who has so many wonderful things to give to this world. If you don't believe it as yet, then believe me. I'm here to tell you *it's absolutely true!*

ABOUT THE AUTHOR

Susan Jeffers Ph.D. is an internationally renowned author and teacher who has helped millions of people overcome their fears and heal the pain in their lives. Her bestselling books include *Feel The Fear And Do It Anyway, Feel The Fear... And Beyond* and *End the Struggle and Dance With Life.* She is also a much sought after public speaker, and media personality. She lives with her husband in Los Angeles.

Visit Susan's website at
www.susanjeffers.com